BUG BOOKS

Earwig

Stephanie St. Pierre

Heinemann Library
Chicago, IL

Customer Service 888-454-2279
Visit our website at www.heinemannraintree.com

Design: Kimberly R. Miracle and Cavedweller Studio
Illustrations: David Westerfield

Color Reproduction by Dot Gradations Ltd, UK
Printed and bound in China by South China Printing Company

12 11 10 09 08
10 9 8 7 6 5 4 3 2 1

New edition ISBNs: 978 1 4329 1239 0 (hardcover)
                     978 1 4329 1250 5 (paperback)

The Library of Congress has cataloged the first edition as follows:
St. Pierre, Stephanie.
Earwig / Stephanie St. Pierre.
        p. cm. — (Bug books)
Includes bibliographical references (p.   ).
ISBN 1-58810-197-5 (lib. bdg.)
1. Earwigs- - Juvenile literature. [1. Earwigs.] I. Title. II. Series.
        QL510 .S72 2001
        595.7'39- -dc21
                                        00-012401

Acknowledgments
The publishers would like to thank the following for permission to reproduce photographs:
© Animals Animals pp. 4 (James H. Robinson), 23 (Tim Shepherd), 26 (OSF/Tim Shepherd); © Ardea (Steve Hopkin) pp. 10, 11; © Bruce Coleman pp. 7 (P. Ward), 9 (R.N. Mariscal), 17 (Jane Burton), 28 (Jane Burton); © Corbis p. 12; © Crandall & Crandall p. 21; © Earth Scenes (Nigel J. H. Smith) p. 20; © NHPA (Stephen Dalton) p. 25; © Oxford Scientific Films pp. 18 (Mike Biakhead), 27 (Satoshi Kuribayashi); © Peter Arnold pp. 6 (Hans Pfletschinger), 8 (Hans Pfletschinger), 15 (AGE), 16 (Hans Pfletschinger), 24 (Hans Pfletschinger); © Photo Edit pp. 19 (Gary A. Conner), 29 (Tony Freeman); © Photo Researchers, Inc. pp. 5, 22 (Simon D. Pollard); © Visuals Unlimited pp. 13 (William Grentell), 14 (William E. Ferguson).

Cover photograph of an earwig on a daffodil reproduced with permission of NHPA (Stephen Dalton).

The publishers would like to thank James Rowan and Lawrence Bee for their assistance in the preparation of the first edition of this book.

Every effort has been made to contact copyright holders of any material reproduced in this book. Any omissions will be rectified in subsequent printings if notice is given to the publisher.

Contents

Some words are shown in bold, **like this**. You can
find out what they mean by looking in the glossary.

What Are Earwigs?

head

leg

thorax

abdomen

Earwigs are **insects**. They have six legs.
Their bodies have three parts. They have
a head, a **thorax**, and an **abdomen**.

antenna

Earwigs are small and flat. Most are
brown. Some have stripes. They have
two long **antennae**.

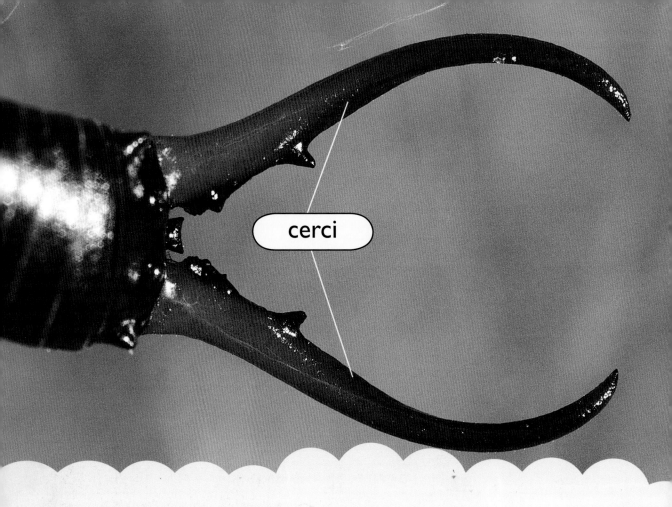

cerci

Earwigs have two large **pincers** called **cerci**. They are at the end of the earwig's **abdomen**.

The cerci are used to fight other earwigs. Sometimes they are used to grab food.

How Are Earwigs Born?

A **female** earwig lays 20 to 50 small white eggs. She lays the eggs just under the ground in winter.

egg

The eggs **hatch** in early spring. The young are called **nymphs**. They stay under ground with their mother until late spring.

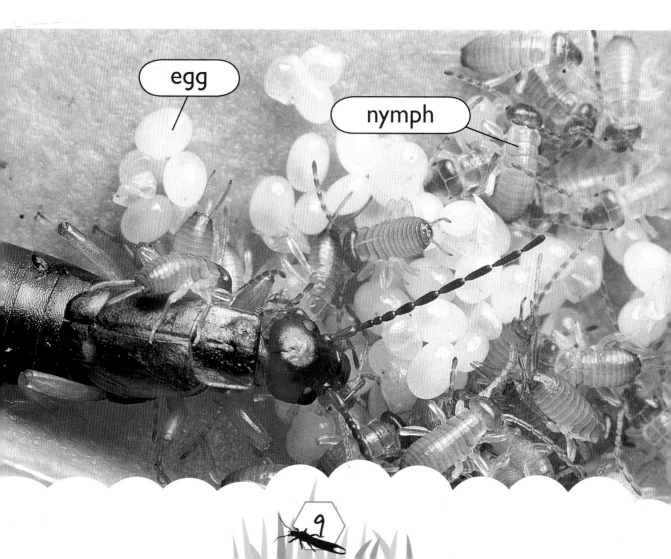

egg

nymph

How Do Earwigs Grow?

The earwig **nymphs** look almost the same as the adults. They are smaller and paler. Nymphs do not have wings.

It takes a few months for an earwig to grow up. As it grows, the nymph gets too big for its skin.

old skin

The **nymph** sheds its tight skin. This is called **molting**. Nymphs molt four to six times before they are fully grown.

As the nymphs become adults their **cerci** become larger. Only adult earwigs have wings.

How Do Earwigs Move?

Earwigs have two wings but they do not usually fly. They move around by crawling.

14

Earwigs can crawl fast but they cannot go very far. They can climb up sticks and stems.

What Do Earwigs Eat?

Earwigs usually eat flowers and plants. They also eat moss, **fungi**, and **pollen**. Sometimes they even eat **insects**, spiders, or other earwigs.

apple

In the summer and fall, earwigs eat fruit. They also like to eat honey from beehives.

Which Animals Attack Earwigs?

Earwigs do not have many enemies. They do not taste good to birds or other **insects**. Some earwigs squirt a bad smell when they are in danger.

The biggest danger to earwigs
is humans. People step on them
or spray them with poison.

19

Where Do Earwigs Live?

Earwigs like **damp**, shady places. Most earwigs live outdoors. You can find earwigs living in flowers or in piles of leaves. They also hide under stones or logs.

Some earwigs live indoors. They hide in cracks near walls. They like damp spots in bathrooms or kitchens.

21

How Long Do Earwigs Live?

Earwigs live for less than a year. They are **nymphs** for two or three months. They live for about eight months as adults.

adult

nymph

Male earwigs usually die in the winter. The **females** look after the eggs and young before they die.

23

What Do Earwigs Do?

Earwigs are nocturnal. This means they sleep during the day. At night they move around and look for food.

Earwigs can damage plants and flowers in peoples' gardens. Some people think they are pests.

What Makes Earwigs Special?

Most **insects** do not care for their babies, but **female** earwigs do. They guard the eggs and bring food for the **nymphs** during the winter.

egg

nymph

Some people think earwigs can climb into people's ears and bite them. This is not true. The **cerci** look dangerous, but earwigs cannot hurt people.

cerci

Thinking About Earwigs

How do earwigs use their **cerci**? Why do you think earwigs might need to fight other earwigs?

Look at this photo and think about
where earwigs might live. Would they live
under the rocks or in the trees? Where
do you think they would be?

Bug Map

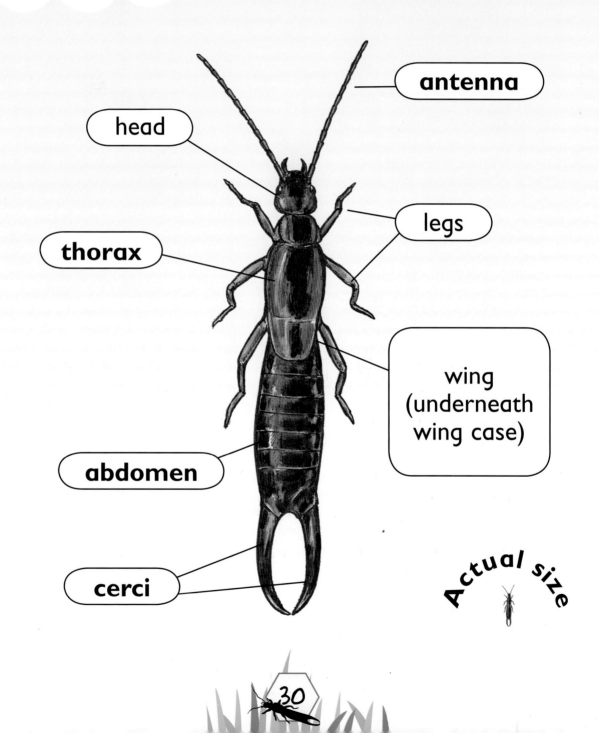

antenna

head

legs

thorax

wing
(underneath
wing case)

abdomen

cerci

Actual size

Glossary

abdomen stomach area at the end of an insect

antenna (more than one = antennae) long, thin tube that sticks out from the head of an insect. Antennae can be used to smell, feel, hear, or sense direction.

cerci (sounds like ser-key, one = cercus) pincer at an insect's tail end

damp little bit wet

female animal that can lay eggs or give birth to young. Women are females.

fungus (more than one = fungi) plant such as a mushroom or mold

hatch break out of an egg

insect small animal with six legs and a body with three parts

male animal that can mate with a female to produce young

molting time in an insect's life when it gets too big for its skin. The old skin drops off and a new skin is underneath.

nymph insect baby that has hatched from an egg. It looks like the adult but has no wings.

pincers part of an insect that can pinch

pollen yellow dust found on plants

thorax middle area of an insect's body, where the legs are attached

Index

More Books to Read

O'Neill, Amanda. *Insects and Bugs (Curious Kids Guides)*.
    New York, NY.: Kingfisher, 2002.
Theodorou, Rod. *Insects*. Chicago, IL: Heinemann Library,
    2007.